Jane Bingham

Heinemann
LIBRARY

www.heinemannlibrary.co.uk
Visit our website to find out more information about **Heinemann Library** books.

To order:
☎ Phone 44 (0) 1865 888066
▤ Send a fax to 44 (0) 1865 314091
▱ Visit the Heinemann Bookshop at www.heinemannlibrary.co.uk to browse our catalogue and order online.

Heinemann Library is an imprint of Capstone Global Library Limited, a company incorporated in England and Wales having its registered office at 7 Pilgrim Street, London, EC4V 6LB – Registered company number: 6695582

Heinemann is a registered trademark of Pearson Education Limited, under licence to Capstone Global Library Limited

Text © Capstone Global Library Limited 2008
First published in hardback in 2008
Paperback edition first published in 2010

The moral rights of the proprietor have been asserted.

Editorial: Sarah Shannon and Robyn Hardyman
Design: Steve Mead and Geoff Ward
Picture Research: Maria Joannou
Illustration: Sarah Kelley
Production: Duncan Gilbert

Originated by Modern Age Repro House Ltd
Printed and bound by Leo Paper Products Ltd

ISBN 978 0431 933 085 (Hardback)
12 11 10 09 08
10 9 8 7 6 5 4 3 2 1

ISBN 978 0431 933 160 (Paperback)
14 13 12 11 10
10 9 8 7 6 5 4 3 2 1

British Library Cataloguing in Publication Data
Bingham, Jane
Ballet. - (Dance)
792.8

A full catalogue record for this book is available from the British Library.

Acknowledgements
The publishers would like to thank the following for permission to reproduce photographs:© Alamy Images pp. **10** (Mary Evans Picture Library), **40** (Jupiterimages/Thinkstock), **42** (Jack Carey); © Corbis pp. **4** (Hubert Boesl/DPA), **13** (Andrea Comas/Reuters), **14, 16, 18, 30** bottom, **35, 38** (Robbie Jack), **19, 22** (Hulton-Deutsch Collection), **20** (Bettmann), **25** (Natasha-Marie Brown/Reuters), **36-37** (Alessia Pierdomenico/Reuters), **39** (Steve Raymer), **44** (Richard Baker/www.richardbakerpictures.com), **45** (Antoine Gyori); © Getty Images pp. **5** (AFP/Pascal Guyot), **24** (Baron), **31** (John Chillingworth/Picture Post), **34** (Photographers Choice/Alvis Upitis), **41**; © Mary Evans Picture Library p. **8**; © Rex Features pp. **15** (Paul Lovelace), **26** (Reg Wilson), **28, 29** (Alastair Muir), **32–33** (Sipa Press); © Topfoto p. **7** (Roger-Viollet).

Cover photograph of Darcey Bussell and Yohei Sasaki in *Song of the Earth* reproduced with permission of © Lebrecht/Laurie Lewis.

Every effort has been made to contact copyright holders of any material reproduced in this book. Any omissions will be rectified in subsequent printings if notice is given to the publishers.

Disclaimer
All the Internet addresses (URLs) given in this book were valid at time of going to press. However, due to the dynamic nature of the Internet, some addresses may have changed, or sites may have changed or ceased to exist since publication. While the author and publishers regret any inconvenience this may cause readers, no responsibility for any such changes can be accepted by either the author or the publishers. It is recommended that adults supervise children on the Internet.

Contents

Some words are printed in bold, **like this.** You can find out what they mean by looking in the glossary, on page 46.

The world of ballet

Ballet is a very special art. At its heart is dancing, but it also involves music, scenery and costumes. When all these elements join together, they create an amazing experience.

Skill and strength

Ballet dancers have to study for many years to learn all their steps and moves. They also have to train their bodies to be strong and supple. The aim of their training is to create dancers who are graceful, skilful and strong.

▼ In traditional ballets, such as *Swan Lake*, ballerinas perform on the tips of their toes. This technique is known as dancing *en pointe*.

In contemporary ballets, dancers use their bodies in exciting ways to express emotions and ideas.

All sorts of ballet

Ballet can be incredibly varied. Some ballets tell a story. Some explore an idea or a mood. There are also ballets with a strong **political** message. In traditional ballets, **ballerinas** usually wear **tutus** and tights, and dance to the music of an orchestra. In contemporary ballets, dancers may be dressed in simple **leotards**, or in striking and unusual costumes. They may use very **acrobatic** movements, and perform to a sound-track of **electronic music**, recorded voices or other sounds.

Whatever kind of ballet you choose to see, the dancers will create a fantastic spectacle. They will use their bodies to make shapes and patterns, as they dance on their own and with other dancers.

Looking at ballet

This book will introduce you to the many aspects of ballet. It starts by tracing the history of ballet from its origins right up to the present day. It looks at how a ballet is staged, concentrating on different elements of a performance, such as **choreography** (the art of creating a ballet), staging and costume. The book also offers advice on how you can train for a career in ballet.

Technique

Turn-out
As soon as they start their training, ballet dancers learn to turn their legs outwards, away from their hips. This special way of standing and dancing is known as turn-out. It makes dancers look very elegant and allows them to perform a wide range of movements. Turn-out is one of the most important **techniques** in ballet. It makes ballet dancers move in a very different way from other kinds of dancers.

Ballet begins

Throughout human history, people have loved to dance. The first dances were probably part of religious ceremonies, but by the time of the ancient Greeks, dancing was seen as a form of entertainment. In ancient Athens, dancers performed the stories of Greek legends. This was the start of a great tradition of telling stories in dance.

Italian dances

After the Greeks and Romans, few people in Europe watched dancing as an entertainment. But then, in the 1450s, some Italian nobles began to take an interest in dance. Dancers performed in grand banqueting halls in front of nobles and their guests. They entertained the diners by telling stories in dance, music and poetry.

Ballet is born

By the 1500s, the fashion for dancing had spread to France, and performances were held at the French royal court. The dancers were all nobles – lords and ladies at court – who were taught their steps by a dancing master.

The French dancers moved together in lines across the floor, in a very slow and stately way. They called this kind of dancing 'ballet' after the Italian word *ballo*, which means 'dance'.

Taking to the stage

By the 1650s, French **court ballets** were being performed on a small raised stage. At the rear of the stage were painted **backcloths** showing beautiful scenery, and the dancers wore elaborate costumes. However, these grand ballets had very little story. They were just a series of dances, linked by speeches and poetry.

Dance Facts

Perfect posture

The nobles who danced at the French court were very proud of their elegant **posture**. They kept their backs very straight and held their heads upright all the time, to support their heavy wigs. The men kept their legs turned outwards whenever they could, so they could show off the shape of their calves. This elegant way of standing and moving soon became a part of the way ballet was performed. Today's ballet dancers copy the posture of the early French dancers!

▼ French court ballets often involved hundreds of performers. Some dances even featured horses!

Ballet for the Sun King

The French king Louis XIV was passionate about ballet, and he played an important part in the history of dance. Louis trained every day with his dancing master. He starred in many court ballets, and he encouraged all his courtiers to join in too.

In 1653, King Louis XIV played the part of the Rising Sun in a ballet that lasted for 12 hours! For this part he wore a magnificent golden costume. The performance was so famous, that Louis became known as the 'Sun King'.

King Louis XIV of France wore a magnificent feathered costume for his role as the Rising Sun.

Creating ballets

King Louis encouraged French composers to write special music for his dances. The composer Jean Baptiste Lully wrote many ballets for the king, and introduced a faster style of music into the ballet. Pierre Beauchamp, Louis' great dancing master, planned the dancers' moves so that they matched Lully's music. He is sometimes seen as the first **choreographer**.

A school for dancers

When he reached his thirties, King Louis gave up dancing and all his courtiers stopped dancing too. But the art of ballet did not die out. Louis had already set up a school for dancers. The school was run by Beauchamp, who gave young dancers a very strict training. This was the end of court ballet, danced by nobles, and the start of a new kind of ballet, performed by **professional** dancers.

Technique

Five positions

Pierre Beauchamp was the first dancing master to teach his pupils clearly defined steps. These steps developed into the five ballet steps that are still taught today:

step 1　　　　　　　　step 2　　　　　　　　step 3

step 4　　　　　　　　step 5

▲ Marie Camargo began dancing when she was ten years old. She was one of the first dancers to use mime.

Women not allowed

By the 1670s, dancers in France were performing for the public in theatres. At first, all the professional dancers were men. People thought that dancing was not a respectable job for a woman, so men wore masks to play the women's parts. However, in 1681 women were allowed to dance in public.

Changing costumes

The first women dancers wore long, heavy skirts, reaching down to their feet. This made it impossible for them to dance as freely as men. Then, in the 1720s, a talented Belgian dancer, Marie Camargo, made a brave move. She shortened her skirt so it came to just above her ankles. This meant she could dance much more difficult steps and show off her speedy footwork.

Over the next few years, male and female costumes became much simpler. Dancers also swapped their hard shoes with heels for soft slippers without any heels. The new ballet slippers gave the dancers much more freedom. Men began to do dramatic leaps, and women performed spectacular jumps and twirls.

Actions not words

Ever since ballet had begun, performances had included singing and speech. But in the 18th century a major change took place. Some choreographers began to create ballets with no words. The ballets were accompanied only by music, and dancers used **mimes** to represent different moods and ideas.

Over the next hundred years, a set of mimed movements were developed that were used by dancers everywhere. Now that ballet no longer needed words, it had become an international art that could be performed all over the world.

Amazing Fact

No more corsets!
In the 1700s, women dancers didn't just have to cope with long skirts. They also had to wear a **corset** under their clothes. Corsets were made from stiff, heavy material and were laced very tightly at the back. In 1734, the dancer Marie Sallé dared to perform on stage without a corset. Soon, other dancers followed her example. At last, women dancers could breathe and move as easily as men.

Romantic ballet

In 1832, a new ballet was performed in Paris. It was called *La Sylphide* and it set a fashion for **romantic ballets**. Romantic ballets are intended to stir people's feelings and emotions, and they usually have a strong fantasy element. They present a world of fairies and spirits, in which the audience can forget their everyday lives.

Tales of magic

La Sylphide tells the story of a young Scottish man who falls in love with a forest fairy, known as a sylph. Some of the ballet's scenes are set in a village and have dances inspired by Scottish country dancing. Other scenes take place in an enchanted forest.

La Sylphide was a huge success, and soon many other romantic ballets were created. Another famous romantic ballet is *Giselle*, the story of a young girl who dies and becomes a spirit. Like *La Sylphide*, it has some scenes set in the real world, and others in a magical, fantasy world.

Technique

Dancing *en pointe*
La Sylphide was written specially for Marie Taglioni, one of the first dancers to dance **en pointe**. When dancers go *en pointe*, they balance on their toes, and arch their feet. This allows the dancer's weight to be carried through the toes, directly up through the bones of the foot, to the knees. Before they go *en pointe*, dancers have to learn the correct foot position. If they do not balance correctly, they can strain their knee joints and push their big toes out of shape.

Dancing in groups

Romantic ballets have many dances for groups of dancers. The group is known as the *corps de ballet*, which is French for the 'body of the ballet'. All the dancers in the *corps de ballet* move together, making beautiful patterns on the stage. In some romantic ballet scenes, the *corps de ballet* is dressed completely in white. These ghostly scenes are known as 'white acts'.

▼ In romantic ballets, **ballerinas** wear beautiful dresses with long, net skirts. Here, a ballerina dances the role of Giselle, a girl who is transformed into a woodland spirit.

Classical ballet

Romantic ballet was very popular with the general public, but some dancers wanted a better chance to show off their skills. In particular, male ballet dancers only had small parts in romantic ballets. Then, in the 1890s, a Russian **choreographer**, Marius Petipa, designed a series of ballets in a new style. This style would later be known as **classical ballet**.

A new kind of ballet

Classical ballets last for several hours, and they are divided into three or four acts. The ballets tell a story, but they also provide plenty of opportunities to show off the dancers' **technique**. All through the ballet there are special displays of skill, known as **divertissements**.

The most famous of Petipa's ballets were *The Sleeping Beauty* and *Swan Lake*. These classical ballets are still great favourites today.

▼ This dramatic scene is from the classical ballet *The Sleeping Beauty*. It is performed by the Royal Ballet.

▲ The 'swans' in *Swan Lake* wear tutus to show off their graceful movements.

Classical style

In classical ballet, female dancers often dance long sequences *en pointe*. They perform complicated jumps and high leg lifts, and they twirl around in multiple **pirouettes**. Male dancers perform incredible leaps and lift their partners high into the air. Dancers also use **mime**, to show the thoughts and feelings of their characters.

Classical costumes

As classical dancers performed more energetic roles, they needed costumes that were easier for them to move in. Men wore tights and short, fitted jackets. Women also wore tights, and a very short skirt, known as a **tutu**. Ballet tutus were made from several layers of stiff net, so they did not cling to the dancers' legs. These new costumes allowed the audience to see the beautiful 'lines' made by the dancers' bodies.

Biography

Peter Tchaikovsky (1840–1893)
Some of the early classical ballets had very unexciting music, and these ballet **scores** have long been forgotten. But one of the first composers for classical ballet was outstanding. He was the Russian Peter Tchaikovsky. He wrote the scores for *The Nutcracker*, *Sleeping Beauty* and *Swan Lake* – three of the most popular ballets ever. Tchaikovsky's ballet scores are full of drama and surprises. They also introduce different musical **themes** for individual dancers.

Famous Dances

The Nutcracker

The Nutcracker is one of the liveliest of the classical ballets. It tells the story of a little girl called Clara who is given a Christmas present of a nutcracker. Late at night, Clara creeps downstairs and finds that her nutcracker and all the other toys have come to life. The Nutcracker Prince leads the toy soldiers in a battle against some evil rats, and Clara helps them defeat their enemies.

As a reward for Clara's help, the Nutcracker Prince takes her on a magical journey through a land of snow to the kingdom of the sweets. Here, the sweets dance for Clara in a series of brilliant *divertissements*. The display ends with a wonderful *pas de deux* by the Sugar Plum Fairy and the Nutcracker Prince. Then, suddenly, Clara finds herself at home again, wondering if it was all a dream.

The Nutcracker Prince and the Sugar Plum Fairy perform a spectacular *pas de deux*, watched by the *corps de ballet*.

Classical dancers

Classical ballets have very large **casts**. Sometimes, there are as many as 80 dancers on the stage at one time. The cast is made up of the **principal dancers**, some **character dancers** and the *corps de ballet*.

Principal dancers

The stars of a classical ballet are the principal male and principal female. These two dancers perform **solos** on their own, and they perform together in a special dance known as a *pas de deux*. In most classical ballets, there are several other principal dancers who dance with the two main dancers and also dance on their own.

Character dancers

Character dancers play important figures in a ballet's story, such as an old father or a wicked witch. They wear very striking costumes and add drama and contrast to the ballet. Character dancers also often provide a strong element of humour, dancing in an exaggerated comic style. They have a different style of dance from the other ballet dancers, and use special moves and steps to display their character.

Corps de ballet

In a classical ballet, the *corps de ballet* has an equal number of men and women. Sometimes they dance with the principal dancers, and sometimes they perform dances on their own. Some of the dances of the *corps de ballet* are influenced by **folk** dances from different countries. These lively dances provide an interesting contrast to the style of the rest of the ballet.

Inspiration from Russia

At the start of the 20th century, audiences in Paris were astonished by a new ballet company from Russia. The company was called the **Ballets Russes**, and it staged short, one-act ballets that combined dance, music and design. The result was a powerful, and even shocking experience unlike anything audiences had seen before. The influence of the *Ballets Russes* spread across the world, and transformed the way that ballet was performed.

Time to change

The first **choreographer** of the *Ballets Russes* was Mikhail Fokine. He was determined to break away from the **classical ballets**, with their long series of **divertissements**. He invented a new kind of ballet that was much more dramatic than before, and concentrated on moods and feelings.

▲ In this modern version of *Scheherazade*, the dancers wear copies of the costumes worn for the ballet's first performance.

Fokine designed short ballets that told a clear and exciting story. Some of his most famous ballets are *The Firebird*, *Scheherazade* and *Petrushka*. *The Firebird* tells the tale of a magical bird-like creature that has to fight against a wicked magician. *Scheherazade* is a collection of stories from Arabia. In the ballet *Petrushka*, a Russian puppet and his friends have some exciting adventures in a fairground.

Vaslav Nijinsky (1890–1950)
Nijinsky was one of the leading dancers in the *Ballets Russes* and he was also a talented choreographer. He was extremely athletic and famous for his enormous leaps, but he also dared to create very unusual movements, such as dancing with flat feet or turned-in toes. In 1913, Nijinsky choreographed and starred in a famous ballet called *The Rite of Spring*. When it was first produced there was a riot in the audience. Everyone was shocked by the ballet's harsh, rhythmic music and by Nijinsky's violent movements. Later, people recognized that the ballet was a work of genius.

▶ Nijinsky was one of the most gifted dancers in history. Here he dances the lead role in *Scheherazade*.

A new style of dance

The *Ballets Russes* introduced a daring new style of dancing. Choreographers such as Fokine still used traditional moves, such as leaps, jumps and twirls, but they also invented some totally new movements to express character and emotion. Some of the new moves were shocking and even ugly.

In the new ballets, there was much less emphasis on balance and **symmetry**, and the **corps de ballet** no longer all moved together. Even though the ballets were often very beautiful, they were much more dramatic and expressive than before, and male dancers were just as important as **ballerinas**.

▶ Anna Pavlova of the *Ballets Russes* here performs the role of Pierrette (a female clown). Pavlova continued to dance right up until her death at the age of 49.

Sergei Diaghilev

The performances of the *Ballet Russes* were not just dramatic dances. They also used stunning costumes, scenery and music to create an exciting atmosphere. The man who combined all these elements was the company's director, Sergei Diaghilev. He had a genius for finding talented people and bringing them together.

New designs

In the early years of the *Ballets Russes*, the company's designer was Leon Bakst. For the ballet *Scheherazade*, Bakst created exotic costumes in brilliant colours made of flimsy material. His designs created a sensation in Paris, and they were even copied by fashion designers.

Bakst's stunning backdrops and costumes were just the start of a revolution in ballet design. Diaghilev soon began to attract all the leading artists of the day to work on his productions. One of the most famous artists to work for Diaghilev was Pablo Picasso, who designed sets and costumes for two of his ballets.

New music

In 1909, Diaghilev commissioned a young Russian composer, Igor Stravinsky, to write a **score** for *The Firebird*. Stravinsky created a driving, rhythmic score that was full of surprises. From then on, Stravinsky worked closely with the *Ballets Russes*. His most famous music was written for *The Rite of Spring*. This powerful score was strongly influenced by the sounds and rhythms of primitive **war dances**.

During the course of his career, Diaghilev invited many composers to write scores for the *Ballets Russes*. The French composers Maurice Ravel, Claude Debussy and Erik Satie introduced a light-hearted and playful mood into ballet music. The Russian composer Nikolay Rimsky-Korsakov drew on lively **folk** music for his inspiration, while another Russian, Sergei Prokofiev, wrote ballet scores that were filled with passion.

Biography

Anna Pavlova

One of the most famous members of Diaghilev's company was the ballerina Anna Pavlova. She was particularly famous for her **solo** ballet, *The Dying Swan*, which was specially created for her by Mikhail Fokine. Anna Pavlova created her own company and toured all over the world. She introduced the Russian style of dancing to millions of people.

New directions

By the 1930s, ballet was developing in many different directions. There were lively companies in Britain, France, Germany, Denmark and Sweden. Ballet was also taking off in America and Australia. All these new companies were exploring new kinds of dancing.

◀ Pearl Primus was an outstanding dancer and choreographer, who founded her own company of black dancers. She helped to introduce a new style of very expressive dancing.

Ballet in America

In 1933, the Russian **choreographer** George Balanchine was invited to set up a ballet company in New York. Balanchine's company later became the American Ballet Theatre. For his new company, Balanchine created **theme** ballets, which developed an idea rather than telling a story. One of Balanchine's most famous theme ballets was *Agon*, a ballet for twelve dancers on the theme of conflict.

While Balanchine was creating his theme ballets, the American choreographer Jerome Robbins was working for the American Ballet Company. Robbins was especially interested in presenting ballets that drew on American culture and traditions. One of his best-known ballets was *Fancy Free*, which told the adventures of three sailors in wartime New York.

New trends in America

Balanchine and Robbins were both closely involved in the development of the first Broadway musicals. Balanchine worked with Richard Rodgers, helping him to create some of his early musicals. In 1957, Robbins choreographed the dance movements for the smash hit *West Side Story*.

By the 1940s, there was a growing interest in the dance traditions of Black Americans. The dancer Pearl Primus created dynamic dances inspired by Afro-Caribbean traditions, and in 1969 the Dance Theatre of Harlem was founded, to develop the talents of black dancers.

Dance Facts

The birth of modern dance

In 1926, a **professional** ballet dancer, Martha Graham, formed a new American dance company. She trained dancers to use their bodies to perform strong, precise movements that expressed powerful emotions. Graham's dance works surprised their audiences by their bleakness and spareness, but they also impressed people with their emotional power.

Martha Graham is often seen as the founder of the **modern dance** movement. Modern dancers use their bodies in a different way from ballet dancers. They do not wear ballet shoes or use classical steps, and their dances involve **acrobatic** movements and **floor work**.

This is a scene from Frederick Ashton's ballet *Daphnis and Chloe*, a love story set on a Greek island. Chloe is danced by the famous English ballerina Margot Fonteyn.

Ballet in Britain

In the 1920s, two remarkable women changed the face of ballet in Britain. They were Ninette de Valois and Marie Rambert, and they had both danced for the **Ballets Russes**.

In 1926, Marie Rambert founded the Ballet Rambert. Then, five years later, Ninette de Valois became director of the Sadler's Wells Ballet, which later became the Royal Ballet. Within a few years, these two companies were performing a wide range of ballets, and introducing new work by British choreographers. They were also training a new generation of dancers.

British choreographers

Britain has produced some outstanding choreographers. Frederick Ashton created ballets from the 1920s until the 1980s. His work includes short theme ballets, such as *Façade*; longer abstract works, such as *Monotones*; and many story ballets, including *Cinderella*, *A Month in the Country* and *La Fille Mal Gardée*. Ashton's ballets are seen as very English in style and are often filled with gentle humour.

Kenneth MacMillan was director of the Royal Ballet from 1970 until his death in 1992. He was not afraid to tackle very difficult subjects, such as the fate of the Jews in World War II. One of MacMillan's best-loved works is *Elite Syncopations*, which presents a set of lively dances, set to jazz music.

David Bintley worked for many years as a **character dancer** but he has always been interested in choreography. In fact, he created his first ballet when he was just 15 years old! Bintley's work includes playful comedies, like *Hobson's Choice* and *The Nutcracker Sweeties*, and powerful story ballets such as *Arthur* and *The Snow Queen*.

▶ Dancers from the Royal Ballet perform Kenneth MacMillan's version of *Romeo and Juliet*. MacMillan emphasises the dramatic elements of this famous love story.

Dance Facts

The Rambert Company
During the 1960s, the Ballet Rambert began to move in a new direction, producing experimental pieces that involved very acrobatic movements. In 1987, the company name was changed to the Rambert Dance Company. This small company of just 22 dancers is famous for creating powerful works on contemporary themes.

Russian masters

In the 1950s, two great Russian ballet companies toured Europe and America. The companies were the Bolshoi and Kirov Ballets, and their dancers astonished Western audiences with their amazing **technique** and passion.

At that time, Russia was a **communist** country and several Russian ballet stars made the decision to stay in the West. The dancer and choreographer Mikhail Baryshnikov worked in Canada and North America, and became artistic director of the American Ballet Theatre. The dancer Rudolf Nureyev was based in Paris but often danced in London, with the English **ballerina** Margot Fonteyn.

▼ The Russian dancer Mikhail Baryshnikov performs in *Rhapsody*, a ballet that was created especially for him. Baryshnikov was famous for his acrobatic leaps.

New moods in ballet

Some modern ballets have a strong **political** message. David Bintley's *Still Life at the Penguin Café* looks at the consequences of human destruction of the environment. In 2006, the American choreographer Paul Taylor produced a powerful anti-war ballet, *A Banquet of Vultures*.

Other ballets contain a strong element of play. The American choreographer Twyla Tharp creates very lively, jokey ballets inspired by jazz and Broadway dance routines. Her most famous ballet, *Push Comes to Shove*, contains many visual jokes about **classical ballet**. The Czech choreographer Jiří Kylián is also famous for his playful pieces. In *Sweet Dreams*, dancers perform bouncy movements with tennis balls in their mouths, while in *Arcimboldo*, the dancers become part of a food fight, as tomatoes are hurled at the stage from the orchestra pit.

Biography

William Forsythe

One of the most exciting figures in ballet today is the American choreographer William Forsythe. He creates ballets for classically trained dancers that require them to twist their bodies into astonishing positions. In his ballet *Steptext*, Forsythe aims to break down classical dance movements to create a new kind of body art.

Dance around the world

Today, there are lively ballet companies all over the world, performing traditional ballets but also creating dances that reflect their national traditions. For example, the National Ballet of China performs classical ballets, but also stages dances such as *Raise the Red Lantern*. This powerful ballet tells the story of a young woman who is forced to marry a cruel warlord. Its graceful movements and dances draw on ancient Chinese traditions.

Creating a ballet

Behind each ballet performance is a huge team of people. As well as the dancers and musicians, many people work backstage, making sure the ballet runs really smoothly. Others are involved in creating the ballet, training the dancers and preparing for the performance. Together all these people are known as the ballet company. At the head of the company is the director, who makes sure that everyone works well together.

All sorts of dancers

Most ballet performances involve a large number of dancers. As well as the **principal dancers**, who dance the main male and female **solo** roles, there are other **soloists**, **character dancers** and the *corps de ballet*. Sometimes, one or more of the principal solo parts are danced by guest stars from another company.

It is quite common for a ballet to have several **casts**, or sets of dancers, who take turns in performing the ballet. This system prevents one cast from becoming too tired. In most ballet companies, each of the main dancers has an understudy, known as a cover, who can dance their part if they are injured or if they suddenly become ill.

▶ Principal dancers must be in excellent physical condition to dance their roles. If they are injured a cover takes over.

▲ The wicked fairy Carabosse in
The Sleeping Beauty is one of the
great female character roles.

Rehearsing for the ballet

Dancers attend rehearsals for several months
before a ballet is staged. The dancers are
taught their steps by a dancing master or
mistress. They have to practise their routines
again and again until they can all dance the
ballet perfectly.

Soloists are coached by a specialist teacher,
called a *répétiteur*. The *répétiteur* works very closely with a dancer,
concentrating on the steps that the dancer finds especially difficult.
Usually, the **choreographer** also plays an important part in the rehearsals,
showing dancers exactly how to use their bodies, and making changes to
steps and movements.

For most of the rehearsals, music is provided by a piano accompanist, but
sometimes dancers practice to recorded music. For the final rehearsals,
dancers perform with a full orchestra.

The art of choreography

The process of staging a ballet starts with the choreographer. The choreographer's job is to create all the steps and movements in a dance. Sometimes choreographers recreate a past performance, but often they invent an entirely new ballet of their own.

Ballet ideas

Choreographers find ideas for their ballets in many different ways. They may read a story that they want to turn into a dance. They may hear a striking piece of music. Or they may be inspired by something in the world around them – such as a flock of birds, or a crowd of people in a street. But whatever their starting point, their next step is to invent a sequence of moves for different dancers.

Music and movement

Music plays a vital part in creating a ballet. Sometimes a ballet is set to music that has already been composed. Then the steps and movements of the ballet have to be carefully matched to the rhythms of the music.

Dance Facts

Inspiration from cinema

The British choreographer Matthew Bourne is often inspired by musicals and films. His *Swan Lake* was influenced by the famous horror film *The Birds*, directed by Alfred Hitchcock in 1963. Bourne's ballet *Nutcracker!* was strongly influenced by the classic film *The Wizard of Oz*.

Matthew Bourne's *Swan Lake* caused a sensation when it was first performed in London in 1995. The ballet is loosely based on the classical ballet *Swan Lake*, but Bourne was also influenced by images from film.

Choreographers often work with a composer, who creates a completely new **score** for their dance. First, the choreographer outlines some ideas to the composer and then the composer comes up with some musical **themes**. Some choreographers and composers work very closely together, creating a new ballet as a team.

Famous Dances

The Green Table

Sometimes, choreographers create a ballet with a very powerful **political** message. In 1932, the German choreographer Kurt Jooss created a famous anti-war ballet, called *The Green Table*. The ballet was staged at the time when Hitler was coming to power in Germany, and Jooss intended his ballet to act as a warning to the German people. *The Green Table* traces the terrible progress of war in eight short scenes. It starts with the meeting of a group of politicians around a green table, and it ends with the final triumph of death.

▲ The 'gentlemen in black' meet around the conference table in a chilling scene from *The Green Table*.

Working with dancers

Dance choreographers are able to imagine what ballet steps will look like. But they also need to try out their ideas with real dancers, so they can see which movements are most effective. Sometimes a choreographer creates a role for a particular dancer, using that dancer's unique skills.

Most choreographers take an active part in rehearsals for their ballets. They work extremely hard with the dancers, making sure that all their moves look just right. It is very common for a choreographer to ask for last-minute changes, even in the final rehearsals.

Choreographers are constantly watching out to see if their moves can be improved. Sometimes they even make changes after a ballet has been performed for some time. Dancers need to be very adaptable, so they can quickly learn a new set of moves.

▲ When dancers prepare for a new ballet, they must learn their roles step by step. They practise again and again until they know every move by heart.

Dance notation

All the steps and movements in a ballet are written down by a choreologist. Choreologists attend rehearsals with the choreographer, and write down each new step as it is explained to the dancers. This exact record is known as dance notation. Later, the dancing teachers use the notation to teach the dancers all the steps of a ballet.

There are many different kinds of dance notation, but the two most widely used are Benesh notation and Labanotation. Most ballet choreologists use the Benesh system (see box), while Labanotation is mainly used for **modern dance**.

Dance Facts

Benesh notation

The Benesh system uses a five-line stave, rather like a music **score**. Each line of the stave represents a different level of the dancer's body: head height, shoulder height, waist height, knee height and ground level. Special symbols are used to indicate the positions of the hands and feet, and body positions are also recorded. The staves are divided into separate sections for each count of the music, so the notation shows exactly what the dancer's body is doing at each count.

Choreologists use a different stave to show each dancer's movements. So, when all the staves are put together, the choreographer can see exactly what each dancer is doing on the stage. A dance notation for a ballet works like a musical score for an orchestra. It shows how all the different parts work together.

▲ In classical and romantic ballets the dancers are usually accompanied by a full orchestra.

Ballet music

There are many different types of ballet music. A ballet score can be flowing and gentle, like the music for the **romantic ballet** *Giselle*. Or it can be full of loud and clashing sounds, like the dramatic music of *The Rite of Spring*. One of the most important elements of a ballet score is its strong rhythm. Ballet music needs to create a very clear beat for the dancers to follow.

Some ballet music is strongly influenced by jazz and rock. For example, in the ballet *Elite Syncopations*, dancers perform some sequences to the jazz music of Scott Joplin. Modern composers for the ballet often use **electronic** musical instruments and recorded sounds to create exciting and surprising effects.

Telling a story

Often, a score helps to tell the story of the ballet. The composer highlights the mood of the story, with loud, fast music for the dramatic, action-packed parts of the story and slow, soft music for the more peaceful scenes. Ballet composers often create a kind of signature tune for each of the main characters. This tune is known as a leitmotiv, and it is played whenever the character appears on stage.

Performing ballet music

Some ballets are performed to recorded music, but often an orchestra plays the accompaniment for the ballet. In many theatres the orchestra plays in a space just beneath the front of the stage, called the pit.

The conductor of the orchestra has an extremely important role in the ballet. It is vital that the beat of the music stays very regular. But the conductor also needs to be aware of the dancers, adjusting the pace of the music if they are having trouble dancing fast enough.

Famous Dances

The Sleeping Beauty

Peter Tchaikovsky composed the music for *The Sleeping Beauty* in 1890. Like all Tchaikovsky's later ballet scores, the music follows a clear pattern. The ballet opens with an **overture**, introducing some of the musical themes that will return later in the ballet. It is then divided into different scenes, each with its own contrasting music.

Some scenes have light and cheerful music, influenced by **folk** tunes. Others have a loud, dramatic accompaniment, to underline the drama of the action on stage. Every time the evil fairy Carabosse appears on stage, the same haunting leitmotiv is played, creating an eerie, frightening effect. The score ends with a grand **finale** of cheerful music, emphasizing the story's happy ending.

▲ In this dramatic scene from *The Sleeping Beauty* Princess Aurora is supported by her parents, the king and queen.

Set design

Once a choreographer has created the story and steps for a ballet, the designer has to start thinking about how the ballet will be staged. Designers make sketches for painted **backcloths** and costumes. They also construct small-scale models of stage furniture, such as thrones and beds, doors, windows and steps. Before they give any instructions for sets to be built, designers create models, to see how each element will work.

Dance Facts

Flying dancers

Set designers can create exciting special effects. In the ballet of *Peter Pan*, some of the dancers have wires fixed to their backs. They leap up into the air, and soar overhead, as if they were flying.

▼ Lighting can be used to spotlight an individual dancer, as in this performance of *Giselle*.

Making the set work

It is very important to make every element of a set work as well as possible for the dancers. Doors, windows and steps all have to be placed very carefully, so dancers can make their entrances and exits from exactly the right place.

Designers also need to create stage furniture that is light and easy to move. Often the furniture is built on wheels so it can be moved very fast between acts. Today, many productions go on tour, so scenery has to be easy to load in and out of trucks.

Lighting the stage

Backcloths, costumes and furniture all help to establish the mood of a ballet. But one of the most important ways of creating mood is by lighting. In some modern ballets the stage is very bare, so lighting is even more important. Lighting designers can flood the stage with warm, red light, creating an exciting, passionate mood. Or they can create a cold, eerie atmosphere with green or purple light.

Lighting can be changed from scene to scene, in order to create a different mood. In a romantic ballet, like *Giselle*, the everyday scenes in the village are brightly lit, while the magical scenes in the forest are much darker. In the forest scenes, dancers are often highlighted by a single spotlight. In the 'white acts', when all the dancers dress in white, lighting designers often create spectacular effects, by using different coloured filters on their lights.

Ballet costumes

Designing and making ballet costumes is a highly specialized art. All the costumes need to look spectacular, and they also need to show the character the dancer is portraying. They must be light and easy to move in, and they have to fit each dancer perfectly. Ballet costumes must also be hardwearing, so they can be worn for many performances.

▼ This spectacular costume was created for the role of the Mouse King in *The Nutcracker*.

Making the costumes

Before the costumes are made, designers need to choose the right fabric, and have it dyed exactly the right colour. At this stage, they need to be aware of how the costume colour will look when it is brightly lit on stage. Some costumes are given special treatment to make them look old, dirty and ragged.

Costumes are created in the wardrobe department. They are sewn on machines and finished by hand. Then each costume is carefully adjusted so it fits a particular dancer's body.

Dancing shoes

The most important part of any dancer's costume is their shoes. Male ballet dancers usually wear soft shoes with no heels known as flats. Female ballet dancers wear special shoes for dancing *en pointe*. In the toe of the shoe there is a section called the toe puff, made from layers of glue and hessian (a kind of thick cloth). Some character dancers wear shoes or boots with heels. The heels make a loud noise when the dancer stamps and kicks.

Ballet make-up

Ballet make-up has to be strong and dramatic in order to show up well under the strong stage lights. All ballet dancers use make-up to exaggerate their features so that the audience can see their expressions. For some parts, dancers wear very striking make-up. They paint their faces and even their bodies to create a totally different character.

Ballet companies have make-up artists who decide how each dancer should look on stage. These experts teach the dancers to do their own make-up. Most ballet dancers allow around half an hour to do their make-up, but some stage make-up takes much longer than this.

▼ Ballet dancers usually apply their make-up themselves, but first they are given lessons by a professional make-up artist.

Training for ballet

The usual starting point for a career in ballet is ballet school. Girls normally start ballet school when they are 11 or 12 years old. Boys begin a little later, around the age of 14. Most students at ballet school have taken ballet classes for many years, and have discovered that they are passionate about dance.

Auditioning for ballet school

Girls and boys who apply for ballet school have an **audition** in front of a group of examiners. The examiners are looking for students who have dancing talent and who respond well to music. Ballet students need to be very flexible, and they need the right sort of body for dancing. Before they can join a ballet school they have to be examined by a doctor to check that they have straight legs, a strong back and the ability to turn their legs out easily at the hips.

▼ Many girls and boys attend ballet classes when they are young. For most of them, dancing is an enjoyable hobby. Only a small number of very talented dancers will go on to make ballet their career.

Life at ballet school

At ballet school, pupils train to be dancers, but they also have to do the same lessons and exams as other school students. Most ballet schools are boarding schools, because the pupils have such long and busy days. Apart from their ballet classes and school lessons, students also have lessons in drama, music and **choreography.**

Ballet students spend a lot of time practising steps and movements. They also rehearse for special school performances. These performances give pupils the chance to dance with an orchestra in front of an audience.

▶ Dancers must work at the *barre* every day, to keep their muscles working well.

Dance Facts

Dance studios

Ballet schools have large dance studios, where the students have classes every day. The studios have mirrors on the walls, so the dancers can check their positions. Dance studios also have a wooden floor, which is slightly springy, to prevent the dancers from damaging their joints. A wooden handrail, called the *barre*, runs around the walls of the studio. Ballet pupils place one hand on the *barre* to steady themselves, when they practice their steps and movements.

Ballet classes

Ballet classes usually follow the same basic pattern. First, the class begins with exercises at the *barre*. These exercises gradually stretch the dancers' muscles and allow their bodies to warm up gently.

After a session of *barre* work, the students are ready to move to the centre of the studio. Here, they repeat some of the *barre* exercises, to help them find their sense of balance. The students also practice different steps and turns, and they work on linking steps together in a flowing sequence, called an *enchainement*.

The last part of the class is usually spent on jumps and travelling steps. During the class, girls concentrate especially on *pointe* work. Boys often spend some time working with weights to build up their muscles for the lifts and jumps.

▲ The boys in this ballet class are practising steps in the centre of the studio.

Dancing careers

In their final year at ballet school, students have auditions to join a ballet company. Most ballet students join a company as part of the *corps de ballet*, but within a few years the most talented dancers will be selected for special training as junior **soloists**.

A few ballet stars move on to become **principal dancers** for a company. These superstars travel round the world, sometimes dancing for their own company, and sometimes taking a starring role in another company's production.

Most ballet careers are very short, as dancers do not usually continue dancing after their mid-thirties. However, many ex-dancers stay in the world of ballet. Most of them become ballet teachers, and some move on to work as choreographers.

Many careers

You don't have to be a **professional** dancer to work in the world of ballet. Ballet companies have an enormous staff, working backstage, promoting the company and offering support to the dancers. People who love dance can also have a very satisfying career working as a ballet teachers and running classes in their local community.

Biography

Darcey Bussell

Darcey Bussell was born in London in 1969. When she was 13 years old, she became a student at the Royal Ballet School, in London. She stayed at the school until she was 18, when she joined the Sadlers Wells Royal Ballet. The following year, she was invited to join the Royal Ballet to dance a leading role in a new ballet. In 1989, when she was 20 years old, she became a principal dancer at the Royal Ballet.

Darcey Bussell has danced all the major classical roles, and has also performed in many modern ballets. She retired from working as a principal dancer in June 2007, when she was 38 years old.

Working backstage

Many people choose to work backstage in a ballet company. They may join a staging or lighting team, or a wardrobe or make-up department. All these jobs require a combination of training courses and hands-on experience. There are also special courses in stage management, and set, lighting and costume design.

Also behind the scenes is a team of specially trained **physiotherapists**. Physiotherapists do not just work with dancers who have been injured. They also help all the dancers to take good care of their bodies and to avoid damaging their muscles and joints.

▲ The job of the lighting designer is a very important one in creating a successful ballet performance.

▲ Working backstage can be very satisfying. Here, an experienced wardrobe mistress adjusts a ballet costume to make it fit perfectly.

Dance degrees

A number of colleges and universities offer degrees in dance. Some of these courses concentrate on performing and teaching skills, and provide an excellent training for teaching dance. Other courses teach choreography and dance notation. Students can study the Benesh and the Labanotation systems of dance notation (see page 33) and take exams that prove they are qualified to record ballets.

Some degree courses prepare students for a career as dance administrators for a ballet company. They make all the arrangements when the company goes on tour and do essential jobs such as organizing ticket sales. Without them, there would be no ballet performances.

Dance for all

Whatever job you choose in the world of ballet, you will be surrounded by people who love dance. They will all be dedicated to producing wonderful ballets, and to helping others enjoy dance too.

Amazing Fact

Billy Elliot could be you!
The film of *Billy Elliot* tells the story of an ordinary boy who achieved his dream of becoming a ballet star. Even though Billy wasn't a real person, there are many ballet dancers with a similar story to his. These dancers started out from small towns with no history of dancing in their family. It is possible to become a leading dancer – if you are prepared to work extremely hard!

Glossary

acrobatic energetic, strong and skilful

audition test to show someone's skill

backcloth large, heavy curtain at the back of a stage that often has a scene painted on it

ballerina female ballet dancer

Ballets Russes Russian ballet company founded in the early 20th century by Sergei Diaghilev

cast all the dancers in a ballet

character dancer dancer who takes the part of an interesting character in a ballet, such as a comic or frightening figure

choreography art of creating all the steps and movements for a ballet

classical ballet type of ballet that tells a story, and is divided into three or four acts. *Swan Lake* and *The Sleeping Beauty* are classical ballets.

communism system of running a country in which all the land belongs to the state, and people have very little freedom

corps de ballet large group of dancers who perform together on stage

corset item of underwear worn by women in the past, to hold their stomachs in very tightly

court ballet type of ballet that was performed in the past by lords and ladies at royal courts.

divertissement short dance in a longer ballet that is meant to show off some of the dancers' special skills

electronic music music produced by instruments such as a computer or an electronic keyboard. Electronic music can include some very surprising sounds.

en pointe ballet dancing on the tips of the toes. Only female ballet dancers perform en pointe.

finale final grand scene in a ballet performance

floor work movements performed by dancers who are using their bodies to make contact with the floor. Floor work is often used in modern dance.

folk music or dance with a long tradition of being used by ordinary people

leotard tight-fitting, one-piece garment often worn by dancers and acrobats

mime silent acting, using movements instead of words

modern dance type of dance in which dancers perform very acrobatic movements to express feelings and ideas. Modern dance began in the 1920s.

overture opening music, performed by an orchestra before the ballet begins

pas de deux dance by two principal dancers

physiotherapist expert who treats damaged muscles and joints, using exercise and massage

pirouette rapid spin performed by a dancer

political to do with the way the world or a country is run

posture the way that people hold their body, and the way they walk and move

principal dancer one of the main dancers in a company, who dances a leading role

professional doing a job as a career. Professionals are paid for doing jobs that many others do as amateurs.

romantic ballet type of ballet that is meant to stir people's feelings and has a strong fantasy element. *La Sylphide* and *Giselle* are romantic ballets.

score written piece of music

solo dance that is performed by just one dancer

soloist very skilful dancer who performs a dance on their own

symmetry perfect balance and matching of different parts of a whole

technique skilful way of doing something

theme idea that runs all through something. Music and ballets can have themes.

tutu short ballet skirt made from several layers of stiff net

war dance dance performed by people preparing to go to war

Further information

Books

Au, Susan, *Ballet and Modern Dance* (Thames and Hudson, 2002)

Bull, Deborah and Luke Jennings, *The Faber Pocket Guide to Ballet* (Faber and Faber, 2004)

Bussell, Darcey and Patricia Linton, *Ballet (DK Superguides)* (Dorling Kindersley, 2000)

Tatchell, Judy, *The Usborne Internet-Linked World of Ballet* (Usborne, 2005)

Films

Billy Elliot (2000)

An 11-year-old boy from a poor mining town discovers he has a talent for dancing. He has to overcome many difficulties before he is finally accepted into the Royal Ballet School.

Center Stage (2000)

A group of teenagers from different backgrounds meet at the American Ballet Academy in New York. Each of them has to deal with the stresses and challenges of succeeding in the world of dance.

The Company (2003)

A young dancer and her friends struggle to succeed within a ballet company. Filmed with the cooperation of the Joffrey Ballet Company of Chicago, the film provides a fascinating inside look at the world of ballet.

Websites

www.abt.org

The site of the American Ballet Theatre. Includes quicktime videos of ballet positions and steps.

www.ballet.org.uk

The site of English National Ballet. Includes features on life behind the scenes at the ballet.

www.australianballet.com.au

The site of Australian Ballet.

www.ballet.co.uk

A very large site providing information on ballet in the UK.

Index